Choosing a Bird

THE AMERICAN HUMANE ASSOCIATION
Pet Care Series

How to Choose and Care for a Bird

Laura S. Jeffrey

Enslow Elementary
an imprint of
Enslow Publishers, Inc.
40 Industrial Road
Box 398
Berkeley Heights, NJ 07922
USA

http://www.enslow.com

American Humane Association™
The nation's voice for the protection of children & animals™

American Humane Association™

The nation's voice for the protection of children & animals™

Since 1877, American Humane Association has been at the forefront of virtually every major advance in protecting children, pets, and farm animals from cruelty, abuse, and neglect. Today we're also leading the way in understanding the human-animal bond and its role in therapy, medicine, and society. American Humane Association reaches millions of people every day through groundbreaking research, education, training, and services that span a wide network of organizations, agencies, and businesses. You can help make a difference, too. Visit www.americanhumane.org today, call 1-866-242-1877, or write to American Humane Association at 1400 16th Street NW, Suite 360, Washington, DC 20036.

To Our Readers: We have done our best to make sure all Internet addresses in this book were active and appropriate when we went to press. However, the author and the publisher have no control over and assume no liability for the material available on those Internet sites or on other Web sites they may link to. Any comments or suggestions can be sent by e-mail to comments@enslow .com or to the address on the back cover.

Every effort has been made to locate all copyright holders of material used in this book. If any errors or omissions have occurred, corrections will be made in future editions of this book.

♻ Enslow Publishers, Inc., is committed to printing our books on recycled paper. The paper in every book contains 10% to 30% post-consumer waste (PCW). The cover board on the outside of each book contains 100% PCW. Our goal is to do our part to help young people and the environment too!

Enslow Elementary, an imprint of Enslow Publishers, Inc.

Enslow Elementary® is a registered trademark of Enslow Publishers, Inc.

Copyright © 2013 by Enslow Publishers, Inc.

All rights reserved.

No part of this book may be reproduced by any means without the written permission of the publisher.

Library of Congress Cataloging-in-Publication Data

Jeffrey, Laura S.
  Choosing a bird : how to choose and care for a bird / Laura S. Jeffrey.
      p. cm.—(The American Humane Association pet care series)
  Includes bibliographical references and index.
  Summary: "Discusses the selection, housing, diet, handling, grooming, and health of a new bird"— Provided by publisher.
  ISBN 978-0-7660-4078-6
  1. Cage birds—Juvenile literature. I. Title.
  SF461.35.J463 2013
  636.6'8—dc23
                                            2011049133

Future Editions:
Paperback ISBN 978-1-4644-0213-5
ePUB ISBN 978-1-4645-1126-4
PDF ISBN 978-1-4646-1126-1

Printed in the United States of America
082012 Lake Book Manufacturing, Inc., Melrose Park, IL

10 9 8 7 6 5 4 3 2 1

Photo Credits: © Angela Hampton Picture Library/Alamy, p. 24; Carolyn A. McKeone, courtesy of Cindy George/Photo Researchers, Inc., p. 34; © Corbis Flirt/Alamy, p. 43; Eduard Kyslynskyy/Photos.com, p. 38; Eric Isselée/Photos.com, pp. 9, 10, 15, 31, 44 (top), 45, © image100, p. 32; Iraida Bassi/Photos.com, p. 25; Mark Stout/Photos.com, p. 1; Michelle Milliman/Photos.com, p. 22; Ramona Smiers/Photos.com, p. 44 (bottom); Shutterstock.com, pp. 4, 6, 7, 8, 11, 14, 16, 18, 19, 20, 21, 26, 29, 35, 36, 37, 39, 40, 41, 42; Stefan Von ameln/Photos.com, p. 12; Tom Tietz/Photos.com, p. 5; © Tony Freeman/PhotoEdit, p. 30; Vitalij Geraskin/Photos.com, p. 28.

Cover Credit: Shutterstock.com (yellow budgie).

Table of Contents

Chapter 1

Great Pets

Birds are great pets. They are social, outgoing, and smart. They enjoy attention, and they will eagerly return affection and friendship. For all these reasons, birds are popular pets. More and more Americans are bringing birds into their homes.

Some people keep pigeons as pets.

Did you know that there are more than nine thousand different types of birds in the world? This is a cardinal.

This book will help you choose the right bird for you. It will tell you what to feed your new pet and how to make it feel comfortable and safe. You will learn how to keep your bird healthy and happy.

Chapter 2
The History of Birds

No one knows when birds became pets. The first pet birds probably were doves and parrots. The ancient Greeks and ancient Romans had pet birds. In India, the mynah bird has been considered sacred for more than two thousand years.

In 1493, explorer Christopher Columbus returned from the lands he discovered with two parrots. He gave them to Queen Isabella of Spain.

The mynah is a very special bird in India.

Birds, such as budgerigars (budgies), are great pets for people who live in apartments or condos because they do not take up a lot of space.

Fast Fact

Larger birds, such as cockatoos, can live to be more than seventy years old. Be prepared to care for your bird for its entire life.

More recently, miners used canaries when they went to work underground. If the canaries passed out, that meant there were dangerous fumes in the mines and that the miners needed to leave right away. Homing pigeons have been trained to deliver messages. Today, millions of Americans have pet birds. Several species have been bred just as pets. They do not exist in the wild.

Birds are friendly and loving. Smaller types of birds usually do not need much space. They also do not cost as much money to care for as other pets, such as cats and dogs.

Birds can live from seven up to seventy years. With proper care and attention, they will give their owners love and friendship for many years.

Chapter 3
The Right Bird for You

A Eurasian bullfinch

Each species of bird has its own unique characteristics. Before deciding which kind of bird to get, think about the following questions: Do you want a quiet bird or a noisy one? Do you want to tame and train your bird? How much time do you want to spend playing and talking with it?

Your answers to these questions will help you decide which kind of bird to get.

Birds like company. These lovebirds, for example, can form strong bonds with their owners. Place the bird's cage where your family spends a lot of time.

If the adults you live with agree, you might think about getting more than one bird. In nature, most birds spend all day with their friends. Unless you spend many, many hours with your bird each day, it should be kept with others of its kind. Otherwise, your bird could become lonely and unhappy.

There are thousands of different kinds of birds found all over the world. They come in all colors and sizes. The most popular birds to keep as pets are parakeets, canaries, finches, cockatiels, and parrots.

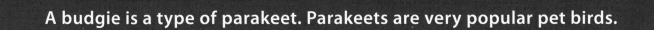

A budgie is a type of parakeet. Parakeets are very popular pet birds.

Parakeets are good for first-time bird owners. Colorful and curious, they are easily trained. They enjoy playing with toys they can push around or climb on. They are very social and can live anywhere from eight to ten years. They like the company of other parakeets, but they may bond to a human more easily if kept alone. You would do well to think about how much time you can give your new bird. Then you can decide how many birds to buy.

The Right Bird for You

Canaries do not like to sit on their owner's finger. They are good pets for people who are looking for a songbird but not a playful friend. Both male and female canaries can sing, but male canaries sing more often and better. With proper care, canaries can live from seven years to fifteen years.

Finches usually do not sing, but they come in many colors and are fun to watch. If you want a cage filled with a lot of activity, think about getting finches. Finches do not do well alone. They should be kept in groups to encourage their normal social behavior. Remember that the more finches you have, the more often you will need to check on their food and water and clean their cage. Like canaries, finches can live anywhere from seven to fifteen years.

Cockatiels are larger and more demanding than parakeets, but they are smaller than parrots. Cockatiels can be easily trained to whistle and talk. They quickly bond with humans, so you should get one only if you plan to spend a lot of time with it. Cockatiels can live ten to thirty years.

Cockatiels are larger than parakeets. They can be trained to whistle and talk.

The Right Bird for You

Parrots are popular because of their size and behavior, but this also makes them very demanding pets. For example, most parrots bond with their mates for life. So when kept as a pet, a parrot will bond very closely with you. Parrots can live anywhere from thirty to seventy years. This means having a parrot is a lifetime commitment—one that few people can keep.

Parrots need constant care, much like the care a baby needs. Without this care, these social birds may become very mean. Parrots are very smart birds. They often need varied activities to keep them busy. Plan to buy toys often and change them regularly. Larger species of parrots can be destructive if left on their own and without toys. They may destroy furniture, curtains, and other household items with their large beaks and claws. They also can be very noisy.

Pet Pointer

Choose a bird that was bred in captivity. Many birds caught in the wild to be sold as pets suffer greatly and have many problems.

Parrots are big, beautiful birds.

Where Should You Get Your New Pet?

Ask your veterinarian or other bird owners you may know to recommend a place. You can get birds from a breeder, who raises birds to sell and knows a lot about their care. Remember that birds are also frequently available from animal shelters and rescue groups.

The most important thing to learn about a bird is if it was bred to sell or if it was caught in the wild. Birds bred in captivity wear a leg band.

Birds that are bred to sell are usually healthier than birds caught in the wild.

When you arrive to buy your bird, make sure all the birds are housed in clean, large cages. They should also have shiny feathers, and their droppings should be firm with both light and dark spots. Be sure that none of the birds in the facility appear to be sick. Birds can easily pass on illnesses to each other.

Chapter 4
Taking Care of Your Bird

A canary

Birds need room to stretch and exercise. So the bigger the cage you get, the better. If you have more than one bird, you should get an even bigger cage. Usually horizontal (across) cages, instead of round or vertical (up and down) ones, give birds the most space to move around in and stretch their wings. The cage should be strong so the bird cannot bend it or tear it apart.

No matter what size bird you get, make sure the size of the cage is right for your new pet.

Taking Care of Your Bird

The bars of the cage should be close together so the bird cannot put its head through them. The paint or finish should be nontoxic so the bird will not be harmed if it pecks it. The bottom of the cage should be removable so that it can be cleaned easily. The cage should have food cups attached to it. Wide food cups are better than deep ones, because birds can see the food better. This may encourage the bird to eat new items.

Food cups should be placed where the birds can see them.

Taking Care of Your Bird

A water cup or dispenser should also be attached to the cage. Some birds also like a getaway spot, such as a nest box, in the cage. Birds also need perches to exercise their feet. Perches come in many types, such as natural perches and rope perches. You can also use dowels as perches. Make sure the perches are not placed where the bird's tail or its droppings will land in the food and water cups.

Use more than one size or style of perch in the cage so that your bird's feet will not cramp. Place one perch near the food and water so the bird can easily get to it. Another perch should be placed high in the cage to give the bird a different view. Finches prefer jumping to climbing. Put perches for finches at each side of the cage so they can jump from one perch to the other.

Birds need perches to exercise their feet.

If your bird becomes upset or is not eating well, move the cage to a quieter area or a new view. These colorful birds are Lady Gouldian finches

Taking Care of Your Bird

Place the cage out of reach of other pets and free from drafts. Make sure your bird has something to see, such as an outside view or people.

Birds eat only during daylight, so put your bird's cage in a bright room. But the cage should not be in direct sunlight. Birds can handle the temperature and humidity that is comfortable for you. They do not like extreme temperatures or sudden changes in temperature. You should not put the birdcage in the kitchen because of the heat and odors, which can be dangerous to birds.

Line the bottom of the cage with white butcher paper. You can also use newspaper, paper towels, or other plain paper. Cage liners to avoid are wood chips, chopped corncobs, kitty litter, or sand. These items make it difficult to see the bird droppings. It is important to see the droppings so you can tell if your bird is healthy. The color and firmness of droppings help tell whether your bird is healthy or sick.

Do not line your pet's cage with cedar, redwood, or pressure-treated pine chips. They can lead to bacteria and mold. Your bird could get sick from breathing them in.

When cleaning your bird's cage, check your bird's droppings. You can ask an adult to help.

Feed your bird food made just for the type of bird you own. Each bird species has different diet needs, so ask a veterinarian about recommended brands, type, and variety for your pet. The three main types of bird food are pellets, nuggets, and crumbles.

You can also feed birds a seed diet rather than specially prepared foods. But you must choose the right kinds of seeds. Make sure the mixture is fresh. Change the seeds daily even when the food cup appears to be full. It may seem full because birds leave behind the empty hulls of shelled seeds.

For birds that eat mostly seeds, the occasional piece of fresh fruit is a sweet treat. This scarlet macaw is enjoying a banana.

Different birds eat different types of food. Budgies eat seeds, fruits, and vegetables. Check with your vet to see which is best for your pet.

Taking Care of Your Bird

Birds on a seed diet need other foods, too. Add fresh, dark green and leafy or dark yellow vegetables. Examples of these are beets, broccoli, carrots, parsley, pumpkin, and sweet potato. Make sure to cut the vegetables into sizes your bird can handle. Celery, lettuce, and other light-colored vegetables are not good for your bird. These foods may cause your bird to have diarrhea because they contain a lot of water. Avocado and uncooked beans can make birds very ill.

Some birds might also enjoy small amounts of fresh fruit, such as cantaloupe, papaya, and apricots. Larger birds might enjoy a slice of apple occasionally. Birds on a seed diet also need protein, such as cooked kidney beans or lentils.

Birds also need calcium, but you should not give your bird milk. Instead, put a shell from a cuttlefish, called a cuttlebone, in the cage. You can also use an oyster shell or a mineral block. These items all provide calcium. Birds will peck at these items to get the calcium they need. Pecking will also cause your bird to swallow small pieces of these items, called grit, which help birds digest their food.

Most birds enjoy a daily bath in a shallow dish placed in the bottom of the cage. They may prefer their bath on a table or countertop outside the cage. Some birds like to have water sprinkled over them. If your bird does not bathe, you can mist it like a plant a couple of times a week. Be sure to keep a wet bird warm and out of drafts.

Birds in the wild spend their days flying, climbing, and jumping. When they are in a cage, they need things to do.

Toys give the birds something to do. Toys also encourage birds to exercise and use their beaks. Avoid toys that the bird can easily take apart, such as small items on link chains. Safe, chewable items for birds include branches, pinecones, natural fiber rope, and soft white pine. Make sure all wood is untreated.

Pet Pointer

Birds like to take baths and showers.

Some birds love to play with toys, such as mirrors and bells. Learn which toys are safe for your bird.

Be sure to change your bird's food and water every day.

Some birds need their beaks trimmed regularly. If the beak grows too long, the bird has trouble eating

Give your bird clean, fresh drinking water every day. Also, change the paper in the bottom of the cage daily. Remove all uneaten fruits and greens, and clean out the food cup. Once a week, take your bird out of its cage and put it somewhere else. Then, scrape the perches and wash and disinfect the cage with a cleaner made just for birds. Rinse everything well so that no soap is left behind. Look for mites or other parasites that could harm your bird.

Chapter 5

Healthy and Happy

An avian veterinarian is a doctor who takes care of sick and injured birds. An avian vet also makes sure birds stay healthy. Take your bird to the vet at least once a year to make sure your bird is healthy.

Birds molt, or lose their feathers, just as dogs and cats shed. When a bird loses its feathers to make room for new ones, it may look shabby and act differently than usual. A normally talkative bird may seem quiet. Also, birds usually will not sing during their molting period.

Healthy cockatiels usually molt about twice a year.

Ask your vet if you have any questions about your pet bird.

During the three to six weeks when your bird molts, treat it as if it were slightly sick. Offer it more sleep, warmth, and possibly even vitamins, but check with your vet before giving your bird any supplements.

Birds have fragile bodies and breathing systems. Everyday household items can harm them. Some pots, pans, irons, and ironing board covers have nonstick coatings on them. These coatings give off chemical fumes when they burn. We cannot see or smell the fumes, but they can harm or even kill birds. Cigarette smoke and bug sprays can also cause breathing problems or serious illness in birds.

To survive in the wild, sick birds try to act normal for as long as possible. By the time you notice that something is wrong, your bird may have been ill for a while. Learn what is normal for your bird so you can easily tell when things are not normal.

Droppings can show changes in a bird's health. Get to know the number, amount, color, and consistency of your bird's healthy, normal droppings. Droppings vary with stress and diet. But a lot of change may show that your bird is very ill.

A healthy hand-tamed bird will like to come out of its cage and be with you.

Other signs of illness in a bird include changes in the feathers, weight, body shape, attitude, personality, behavior, eating or drinking habits, or breeding. Other signs are bleeding, vomiting, or discharge from the nostrils, eyes, or mouth.

A sick bird sits quietly with its feathers puffed up. Do not confuse this with a bird that is just resting or taking an afternoon nap. A sick bird usually stays fluffed up at the bottom of the cage and does not eat. Other problems to be aware of are mites and lice. Mites and lice are parasites. They live on or in the skin and feathers. Many products to control parasites are available, but not all of them are safe. Ask an avian veterinarian for the best brand and how to apply it.

Fast Fact

If your bird is not eating or moving around much, call the vet.

A healthy bird is a happy bird.

Parrots and other birds may also get a disease called psittacosis or "parrot fever." Parrots with this disease may sneeze, cough, and shiver. Their feathers look ruffled, and they may have diarrhea. Many birds die from the illness, but others get better. Healthy birds can be carriers of the disease. They infect other birds as well as people. People get it when they become exposed to bird discharges and droppings.

People with parrot fever feel as though they are coming down with the flu or pneumonia. They have chills, fever, headache, and a cough. Parrot fever may be mild or severe, but it is rarely fatal in people. It is important to call a doctor quickly to get proper treatment.

Pet Pointer

Keep your bird's cage clean to help it stay healthy.

Chapter 6

Preventing Problems

Birds are very smart. They need things to do to keep them happy and healthy. The best thing you can do to prevent problems is to play and talk with them every day.

Depending on what type of bird you have, you may want to let it out of its cage often to stretch its wings. Make sure you always know where your bird is. Turn off ceiling fans because birds cannot see the turning blades. Keep windows and curtains closed. Birds cannot see the glass.

Cockatoos need a lot of attention.

Birds can be let out of their cages. Some can be trained to remain on their perches.

If you let your bird out of its cage, make sure you always know where it is. African gray parrots are very smart, but it is still up to you to keep your bird safe.

They may injure themselves trying to fly out a closed window. Ask your avian veterinarian about clipping your bird's wings to prevent escape or injury.

Make sure there is no soapy water in the sink. Breathing it can be toxic for your bird. Many birds have drowned in dishwater left in the kitchen sink. Also, when your bird is loose, make sure no one is frying or cooking in the kitchen. Birds do not realize the danger of the heat or spitting oil.

Check the tops of doors before closing them. A perching bird might not be able to fly off in time. Also, hide houseplants, which may be toxic. And do not forget to keep an eye on other household pets, such as dogs and cats.

You can train some birds to sit on your finger

Chapter 7
You and Your New Bird

Canaries can be entered in singing competitions.

After you bring home a bird, or several birds, you will enjoy spending time with your new friends. You can talk to them, play with them, train them, or just watch them. But there is even more you can do. Some people become involved in social activities with their birds. They join clubs for bird owners. They even attend bird shows, where birds compete for prizes.

You and Your New Bird

For example, there are singing contests for canaries. Canaries like to sing at daybreak. So the birds are kept in dim light until it is their turn to perform.

Remember that depending on what kind of bird you get, your pet can live to be more than seventy years old. Get more information about your new pet at the library or on the Internet. Ask an adult to help you. Enjoy your new pet bird or birds!

Keep loving and learning more about your bird, and you will spend many happy years together.

Life Cycle of a Bird

1. All birds lay eggs. A baby bird usually takes several days to peck its way out of the shell.

2. After a few weeks, a bird will grow feathers and be able to fly.

3. A full-grown bird may live between seven and seventy years.

Words to Know

avian—Having to do with birds.

breed—To control when an animal reproduces; a group of animals with similar features.

canary—A small, yellow bird that originally came from the Canary Islands.

cockatiel—A small parrot with a long tail and yellow head.

cockatoo—A parrot that originally came from Australia and the East Indies. It usually has white feathers with a yellow or pink tint.

cuttlebone—The inside shell of a cuttlefish, used with food for caged birds. A cuttlefish is an ocean animal related to octopus and squid.

dropping—Waste, or dung, from animals. In birds, droppings contain both their solid and liquid waste.

parakeet—A small, thin parrot with a long tail.

Read More About Birds

Books

Glover, David, and Penny Glover. *Owning a Pet Bird*. North Mankato, Minn.: Sea to Sea Publications, 2008.

Hamilton, Lynn. *My Pet Bird*. New York: Weigl Publishers, 2009.

Kawa, Katie. *Playful Parakeets*. New York: Gareth Stevens Publishing, 2011.

Internet Addresses

American Humane Association
<http://www.americanhumane.org/>

ASPCA Kids: Bird Care
<http://www.aspca.org/Home/ASPCAKids/
Pet-Care/bird-care.aspx>

Index